Tales from a Crowded Pet Room

(A Guinea Pig's Observations of Life with Kids)

No embellishment was required in the writing of this story.

THERESA CONES

ISBN 978-1-64003-072-5 (Paperback)
ISBN 978-1-64003-073-2 (Digital)

Covenant Books, Inc.
11661 Hwy 707
Murrells Inlet, SC 29576
www.covenantbooks.com

CONTENTS

ACKNOWLEDGMENTS

To my husband, John, and daughter, Katie for convincing me to publish our family's story. Katie, I will never forget the encouraging post-it note trail you left from the garage to my computer, where you had various publishing websites loaded for me to research.

To my parents, Lou and Micki, who never wavered in their belief that I could and should finish this book.

To Dr. Stacie and Kristen from Prosper Family Eye Care who never gave up or doubted that Katie's vision could be restored. They were my rock during the hard times.

And finally, to Petsmart for selling us the two cutest, most amazing guinea pigs ever!

PREFACE

M any people wondered what in the world gave me the idea to write a book from the perspective of a guinea pig! It actually came about because of an unusual string of events that life sometimes throws at you.

At the end of Katie's third grade year in school, we started noticing some things were academically challenging for her. After a bit of testing that summer, we had a few answers. It seems Katie had multiple visual processing issues and, in addition, had no peripheral vision to speak of (18-degree field instead of the normal 210-degree field). During this time of therapy, exercises and doctor appointments, the pets provided welcome relief from the stress. At times, they provided so many challenges but other times, I would walk into the pet room and smile at the creatures God had created, then feel an instant peace.

One of Katie's exercises was called, "Moving Window." She had to read a story as a bar went across each word and the computer timed her pace. She hated this because the stories were so boring. One day, she asked if I could write a story and paste it into the computer program. After some research, I realized this was possible (and time consuming), and asked what would interest her. She said she'd like to read about what the pets do while she was at school all day and so the idea was hatched. Every day, I'd try to write a few pages to have ready to paste into the computer program for that night. It was long work but she seemed much more interested in reading about Sarah's adventures than the size of a whale's stomach.

In hindsight, we often think that perhaps Katie's love of pets came from her vision issues. They provided such comfort and love, and she was able to use her imagination so much while playing with them. We continued to work on therapy after the move to Texas, and never stopped praying about her peripheral vision coming in. One day, in July of 2015 our prayers were answered! As she was barrel racing she went around one barrel and saw a miniature horse out of the corner of her eye. After the next barrel, she saw the arena out of her side vision! That night at volleyball something else strange happened. The umpire threw the ball up the court to the server and she saw it go by! Then, as we drove down our street, she noticed that she could see grass and houses, not just mailboxes! Several days went by before she even brought this up; she described all these strange things to me and asked what they meant.

I got the chills as I did a few quick exercises to check her field of vision. And just like that, our Katie had normal peripheral vision! This was truly a miracle that God alone could provide. The doctors were stunned but ecstatic, as were we! So many things changed so quickly after that, and the progress she made was simply amazing. She started enjoying sports and school like never before, and it was so fun to be along for the ride.

Sarah died shortly after this time, and I can't help but marvel at the timing. She had been with us for the entire journey and we missed her terribly. I had stopped writing the book during the move but felt compelled to finish her story, even if it is was through Molly's eyes. I hope you enjoy their story.

> *Genesis 1:25 God made all sorts of wild animals, livestock, and small animals, each able to produce offspring of the same kind. And God saw that it was good.*

CHAPTER 1

My Family

Hello there, my name is Sarah, I am a beautiful sable and white Guinea Pig. I live with my sister, Molly, in a crowded pet room with our family of humans. I am quite possibly the most loved (and overstimulated) guinea pig you may ever meet. The overstimulation is a direct result of my kid owner, Katie, who also lives in this house. She is eight years old, and is always looking for an adventure that involves me and Molly.

We live in Charlotte, NC with Katie, and her eleven-year-old brother, Austin. They love us to the moon and back, which can be good or bad, depending on the day. There is also an older batch of adults that seem to tell them what to do, their real names are John and Theresa. For some odd reason, Katie calls them "Moozie" and "Dadzers," so that's what we call them too. Moozie is the one that remembers to feed us, change our water, and clean the cage, (she also calls us "poop factories" but I'm not sure why). Moozie seems to be the voice of reason when Katie takes us for a ride in the Crazy cars, or in her bike basket, so we really like Moozie. We share our room with three parakeets, Little Anne, Blue and Angel, and two turtles, Speedy and Spring. At night, the family's Golden Retriever, Bailey is locked in with us to make sure we stay in our cages (I guess). We also have an Aquarium that has both frogs and fish we can watch so it's really quite a nice setup. But it hasn't always been this way.

I should digress and give you a bit of background about Katie before I go any further. Although she is an adorable child, people often use the words "strong-willed" to describe her. (I think that means that she won't give up on an idea once it's in her head.) Katie told me of her plan to sleep with Abby, the family's beloved Golden Retriever, before I came along. Moozie thought that wasn't sanitary, and hated the idea of all the hair on Katie's bed. So guess what she did? Katie decided to sleep on the floor with Abby. At first, the parents thought it was a fleeting idea and soon she would return to her bed...but after 6 months of sleeping on the floor with her dog, Moozie began her first in a long string of "giving in to Katie." That child is persistent!

Katie sleeping with Abby

Well, back to the story. Katie has accumulated her collection of pets quite suddenly, mostly during the last 12 months. Apparently, when her parents moved her from New Jersey to Charlotte, she only had two measly pets. The family was very sad because they had just lost Abby[1] (at age 12), and all they had left was a Springer Spaniel puppy (Miles) and a different, less fortunate guinea pig named Darwin.

Miles with Stinky Bunny

---

[1] Abby was our Golden Retriever in New Jersey, and Katie's first dog. She died at age 12 two weeks before we moved to Charlotte.

Darwin on Picture Day in New Jersey

It was a rather abrupt move because of a horrible, freak snow storm that hit New Jersey during the fall of 2011. Six inches of snow covered everything, and it was still October! This caused quite a problem for moving since they were forced to pack in a dark, 46-degree house and leave without even saying goodbye to any of their friends from school. My family arrived in North Carolina exhausted and soon began the process of settling into their rental house.

All was good for several weeks until Darwin ate some bad hay (I live in fear of that, personally) and suddenly fell over—dead—while Katie was at school. Moozie was not happy with that discovery, I can promise you that! Anyway, Moozie must have really liked guinea pigs, because she picked the kids up from school and promptly took them to Petsmart. And guess what? She said guinea pigs are so much fun that each kid should get to pick out their own! Actually, what I think she said was "A guinea pig makes a great pet if you have to own a rodent" but whatever. So Katie picked me and Austin picked Molly, and off we headed to our new home!

Austin with Molly, Katie with me at Petsmart!

We were so eager to see if they would pet us or pay attention to us, (we had heard some rumors in the cages about guineas being ignored by their kid owners so we were worried). Well, that did not happen to us, in fact, quite the opposite happened. This is the story of our adventures during our long and crazy lives living with Katie, her family, and her other pets. I will tell you that watching Katie grow from a spunky eight-year-old to an almost thirteen-year-old has been the ride of a lifetime, I hope you enjoy it as much as I enjoyed living it!

CHAPTER 2

Life in the Cones' Household

Well, we arrived home from Petsmart to quite a welcome reception from Miles. It appears he had not been briefed on the proper way to greet guineas without scaring the hay out of them (literally) and this was going to be a problem. Molly and I started to wonder if Darwin really died from bad hay or a heart attack, but I think heart attacks are very rare in young guineas.

Anyway, back to Miles. He was really quite ill-behaved, but for some reason it didn't really bother my humans. They let him smell us, take naps right next to us, bark at our cage, and even allowed him to lick us! We were very disturbed by their lack of Guinea manners but felt powerless to change the situation. We lived for nice, sunny days when Moozie would take Miles in the yard and throw the tennis ball to him for hours. Luckily, he'd come back exhausted and we would get the afternoon off.

We inherited Darwin's cage, which was plenty spacious for one guinea, but we both knew we would need more space soon. That was on the top of our list to address with Katie, since she seemed to be the one that talked her parents into all the big purchases. We had a ramp, an igloo and a tunnel to crawl in (and hide from Miles) so for the most part we were happy.

Our days were filled with lots of activity. We would eat, drink, eat, poop, and then sleep in our Igloo. It was very relaxing, until about 3:30 when my kids would get home from school. Katie would head right to the cage and scoop us up and take us out to the swing set to slide down the slide. (I'm fairly certain this is strictly discouraged in the Guinea manual but that didn't stop her.) Sometimes she would forget we were playing with her and leave us on the playground mulch all alone. Luckily Moozie would come out and remind her that there were hawks in the area and that wasn't a good idea. We love Moozie!

Other times, Katie would put us in a ferret carrier and walk around the neighborhood with us, which felt a little like being in the backseat of a car on a winding road. I'm so happy guineas aren't prone to nausea or things would not have been pleasant most days. Katie loved it, though, which is all that seemed to matter as we were rarely consulted on activity choices.

Our cage in the rental house was on a landing upstairs, so we had a great view of all the activity around us. It was also a great place for us to toss up litter that would fall down into the family room, which seemed to make Moozie crazy. She must love to sweep, because twice a day she would scoop all our discards into a dust pan while muttering how filthy rodents can be. We personally found that offensive and would pretend we didn't understand what she was saying.

We also have a secret about Moozie. No matter how much she says she doesn't like us, when the kids are at school she gets us out of the cage and holds us on her lap while she's working on her computer. None of her friends seem to know this, so we don't tell them. Guineas are very good at keeping secrets.

CHAPTER 3

Picture Day

"Oh no, Molly, come quickly! Katie has that look in her eyes." As I feared, today is "picture day." Every month we have picture day and for the first step, we are always taken to the "Guinea Pig Spa" in her bathroom (against our will I might add!). It sounds nice for a girls' trip, but believe me we hated the spa! Unfortunately, it appears there will be multiple services on the agenda today, all of which are hated by guineas.

Katie starts in the washing station where she gives us a bath followed by "drying" us (i.e. squeezing a towel tightly around us for about 10 minutes). We are totally immobilized and shaking with fear, which she thinks means we are shivering. We are rushed to the drying station, (which is a chair with a seat belt for a doll), strapped in, and then the hair dryer goes on full blast (more shivering from fear). Luckily, Moozie hears the hair dryer and runs in to save us! Where was she during the bath? When we are sufficiently dry, we head to the perfume station (it's hard to get rid of rodent smell).

Next, it's dress-up time followed by hair bows being plastered on our heads (very embarrassing!). Unfortunately, Katie got most of these ideas from the movie, G-Force, but I'm not sure she realizes those guinea pigs weren't real. Once we are dressed, we head to the picture-taking area (the shower) and she gives us our choice of backgrounds. We fearfully step into the shower in front of the blue backdrop and begin to smile while the flash goes off repeatedly. She's a great photographer, always engaging us in the action with squeaks and squawks that are supposed to mimic us (she is actually amazing at guinea noises). Unfortunately, our eyes are almost always red in the picture, so she gets frustrated and keeps taking more pictures... same result. She really needs to learn about photo editing very soon.

As we head downstairs, Katie is shouting, "Mom we have some pictures to print!" and I hear Moozie sighing. (We can only hear her since we are temporarily blind from all the flash photography.) No way is she more tired than we are, I'm so glad Picture Day only happens once a month. Once we are back in the cage, I sleep for 3 hours.

This is me (above) and Molly on Picture Day.
You can see that I chose a bow, Molly went plain.

CHAPTER 4

Birds and an Angel

Back in September, Katie started telling her Mom that if she could only get a parakeet she would be so happy and she'd never need another pet. "No, no and no" was all I heard from her parents (they are very smart; I think birds are just flying rodents). Katie continued on with quite a bit of persistence until it was almost Christmas time, then she went full throttle with the begging. I was so proud of Moozie, she kept saying "No!" Finally, one day when Moozie was really tired, she said "Ok, if you can bring 5 of your "Good" scores up to "Excellent" on your report card, we'll think about it (Moozie was smiling inside because Katie really doesn't care much for school).

Boy, did we all underestimate Katie. Part of the problem was that in second grade she had the most amazing teacher named Miss Maye, and she really wanted to impress her. She started really applying herself and actually working on her homework. No one had anticipated this turn of events. By January, Moozie was pretty worried; it looked like she was going to get some "Excellent" marks!

One day, while we were looking at the computer together (I was nestled on her lap but don't tell anyone), I saw Moozie shopping for bird cages at Petsmart! "No!" I shouted, "Don't you realize how disgusting birds are? Molly and I are not sharing a room with them!" Pretty soon, Dadzers walked in and she showed him the cages, and reminded him Katie's birthday was coming up and maybe they should surprise her. We were crushed but powerless to stop it. The day the birdcage arrived was a somber day in our pet room.

Two weeks later, the entire family was back in Petsmart picking out a parakeet but there is a slight problem. The sign says they are "social animals" that live in colonies (paraphrase: it would be cruel to just get one). The kids poured it on thick, reminded her that Austin had good grades too so he should get to pick one as his pet. Somehow, they came home with a green one (Little Anne) and a blue one (Blue).

They are such annoying creatures, every morning at 8:30 they chirp for a solid hour which really gets on my last nerve. Soon, we all settle in together, and Molly and I try to play nice but we don't appreciate the attention-stealing, flying rodents one bit. During this time, Katie starts telling her mom that she really wishes she would have gotten an all-white bird, I mean, "blue and green are pretty but white reminds her of angels!" This continues for weeks, and slowly starts to intensify during visits to Petsmart. Katie bravely asks the sales person if you can add a bird to your cage when you already have two at home (Moozie had told her they would fight and it's not possible, Katie did NOT like that answer). The unhelpful sales person told her that "Yes, you almost always can as long as you don't wait too long. If you just got your birds, you better decide pretty soon". Thank you very much for that answer!

Unfortunately, Easter rolls around, and some unknowing family member gives Katie a $50 gift card to Petsmart. Moozie tried, she really did, but within a week the third bird, named Angel, arrived. Even still, Moozie and Dadzer were very happy because they just knew she is now going to be content, right?

CHAPTER 5

The New House

Several months flew by and, all the while, no word on the new house they were trying to buy (it was a slow process). Moozie was so busy with all the details that she kind of forgot about us for days at a time, which was not pleasant. Finally, it was time to close on our house, and our new life was about to begin. We were so excited!!

As the moving trucks came, we all loaded into the minivan and drove the 5 miles to the new house. And guess what? We had our very own pet room! Well, maybe it wasn't exactly a "pet room;" I think it is actually the kids' "homework room" but that is just a detail. Our new room had two windows (odor control) with desks that the kids were supposed to work at. Moozie quickly realized that when you have a kid like Katie, putting her in a room with all her pets is not conducive to homework completion. Once she figured this out, it was too late, by then there was no other place to put all our cages!

We loved our new area, but we really hated being right next to the birds! Sometimes, when Katie would go to school she would leave their cage open. I can't tell you how many times all three of them would land on the wire roof of our cage and torment us. Not only that, they were dropping bombs all day that we had to jump to avoid! (And Moozie says we are poop factories?) It was disgusting and we were not happy about it. We would look at the open window and wish Katie would forget to close the cage door, just once. I kept telling Katie, "If you love something set it free......" but she acted like she didn't hear me. Molly and I REALLY think the birds would be happier living in the wild.

Back to our pet room…the great thing about having all your pets in one area is that the mess, noise, food, supplies and cages are all in one room. (The bad thing about it was that all the mess, noise, food, supplies and cages are all in one room.) This seemed to really bother Moozie, she likes order and the pet room was definitely not orderly! Every day she would have to light a candle or open the windows for "odor control," whatever that means. We thought it smelled great, but Moozie was always muttering about how she can't believe she has so many "stinky" pets. Some days she looks really tired, and we promise each other we'll be cleaner and better for her but it's so hard to take the rodent out of a rodent.

When Moozie had to leave, she would lock Miles in the room with us and we'd all talk about our day and eagerly anticipate Katie's return from school. We never knew what adventures we would be facing at 3:30 PM. During these talks, we started to realize that Miles was a little freaked out about the move; and it seemed he still missed Abby (it had been 4 months but he was very fond of her). He loved the new house and having a fenced-in yard, but something seemed to be different with him. Molly and I couldn't figure it out but we were concerned. We both hoped he would snap out of this mood quickly.

CHAPTER 6

Miles and Bailey

As the weeks passed, we continued to worry about Miles. His behavior had always been deplorable, but it was getting even worse. He loved Austin and Katie, and lived for chasing the tennis ball but something was wrong. He was starting to act a little crazy when kids came over, barking at them as if he was really frightened of them. His actions became more aggressive, and Moozie was NOT happy. I mean, way too many kids come over for her to be worried about what Miles would do (see, aren't Guinea Pigs the perfect pet?). Well, I digress, back to Miles.

As the weeks turned to months, it was apparent there was a very real problem. One day, a five-year-old girl came to play and when she tried to pet him, he snapped at her! It didn't break the skin, but Moozie was beside herself! It was obvious he was not comfortable in a home with kids. The next day she started doing some research, and found a Springer Spaniel rescue group that was created just for this type of problem. As I sat on her lap, Moozie tearfully began searching for the perfect home for him (she REALLY loved Miles). I don't mind telling you that I have never seen her cry as much as she did during the next few weeks. I honestly think she liked that ill-mannered dog more than me and Molly, which is very hard to fathom.

The worst part was telling the kids, which did not go so well. Talk about a guilt trip, the kids laid it on so thick and made Moozie feel like the cruelest mom in the world. It really tore me up to watch

Moozie drop them off at school, and then come home and hold Miles, and just sob for hours. During this time, Moozie and Dadzers decided they must go back to owning a Golden Retriever; they were never going to worry about giving away another dog! So 3 weeks before Miles was scheduled to go to his new family, Bailey arrived!

Bailey, already in a Katie-created costume, day 2

It pains me to say this, but that little puppy was pretty darn cute. And guess what? She loves guineas! Or at least, she loves eating our food and hay. Katie has made it her mission to make sure we are friends, even if she has to force us. Some days she has us walk side-by-side on the leash which is challenging given our height and speed differences. Other times she puts us on Bailey's back so we can go for a "horse ride." Apparently, she doesn't notice our "fear" shedding during these times of forced camaraderie. But as you know, Golden Retrievers are gentle creatures and, even though she is still a little crazy, I think we are going to like growing old with Bailey.

One of Bailey's worst traits as a young puppy was car sickness. If she wasn't drooling in the car, she was vomiting. Moozie hated that! The vet recommended more car trips to resolve the problem, starting with quick errands. One day, when the kids were at tennis camp, her mom decided it was the perfect first trip to bring her on. As she was driving, she could hear Bailey in the back seat throwing up but thought "how much can a little puppy vomit?" Soon she was at camp and forgot all about the "little pile" that must be on the back floor. Katie and Austin jumped in and started hugging on cute little Bailey. Soon Katie exclaims "Oh gross, did Bailey eat spaghetti?" "What?" I say. "There is a pile of spaghetti on the floor back here, and it's moving!" Now Moozie starts to really freak out! "Austin, is that true?" Well, long story short, it was true and it was disgusting. The trip home was diverted to the Vet for another dose of worm medicine, but Moozie was not thrilled to clean the floor mat that afternoon! This is a good time to mention again that guinea pigs don't get worms, and are the perfect pet.

Another thing Katie decided was that even though Bailey is a female, she looked a lot like a "Bubba," so she informally changed her name. (Katie is big on name changes.) Eventually everyone was slowly forced to call her "Bubba" if Katie was around, which was a little strange. Luckily, Bailey doesn't come no matter what you called her, so it didn't really affect her behavior.

There was only one tiny problem with Bailey; she started to grow. And she grew, and grew. Soon Katie started subtly mentioning that Bailey was getting too big, she had really wanted a puppy "that would stay a puppy forever." The more Bailey grew, the more frequent Katie's comments became and Moozie started to get concerned. She was determined that this house was going to be a "one dog" house. No matter how many comments Katie makes about wanting another dog, they are NOT going to give in. We shall see.

CHAPTER 7

Speedy and Spring

Shortly after Miles left, my family headed off to Hilton Head and, although they had to leave Bailey home, they brought us! Katie insists that Guineas love being crammed into a cat carrier, and taken on a car ride that makes them shed for 4 hours from total fear. After arriving, we were exhausted but soon learned that no pets were allowed in the house they are renting. That was very troubling, but somehow Katie convinced Moozie that we don't really count as pets and should be easy to sneak in. We were a little uncomfortable with this, but no one asks what we think.

Anyway, Hilton Head is such a lovely island with so many things for a Guinea to do that we had a great vacation. And guess what the best part was? The rental bike that Katie got didn't have a basket, so we missed all the bike rides! That is always a relief. As fun as it sounds, I really had no interest in riding through the waves on the beach, just waiting for a hungry pelican to grab me!

Every day, when my family would go to the beach Katie would pass a store that had a sign for "free turtles." "Wow, can you believe that Moozie? They're free!" (That is after you pay $24 for the cage and food, but details are not important to Katie.) At first, Katie just made comments about how cute turtles were. Slowly the intensity built, and by the end of the week you would have thought turtles were the most amazing animals ever created. I kept telling Moozie all the reasons she needed to say no, but to no avail. I mean, for starters, it is illegal to sell them in South Carolina (that is the reason they are

28

free and you pay for the cage). I am pretty sure if Moozie knew she was committing a crime, we could have stopped this fiasco.

Another issue with turtles is that they carry Salmonella, how disgusting! I am not aware of even one disease that guineas carry, but you don't hear that on the news. Once again, I was overruled and by the end of the week we had a turtle named Speedy, riding home next to us in the car. Molly and I both let him know we thought he was disgusting but he pretended to ignore us.

When we got back to the pet room Katie realized that the tiny cage he had come in was more of a "travel cage" and we needed a bigger tank. Off to Petsmart they went, and came back with all sorts of supplies for the "free turtle" who now has cost $100. Moozie is a saint I tell you! Anyway, the only good thing about having Speedy was he was a nice diversion and we got some much needed rest. When Katie's aunt came to visit, she suggested that every day, Katie should fill the bathtub and let him swim to get exercise. Katie embraced that idea, and created a tropical habitat in her bathtub. This soon became a time-consuming, mess-creating activity that Moozie got to deal with, but at least Speedy and Katie were happy.

Speedy went everywhere with them, even on the 1,000 mile car trip they took twice a year to Texas. I mean, who doesn't travel with a turtle, two Guineas and a very car sick dog twice a year? I'm starting to understand why all of Moozie's friends think she's crazy.

29

The months pass and Easter comes, and back to Hilton Head they go, only this time I had to stay with a pet sitter! Before she left, I made Katie promise that she would not bring back another turtle, but I think she had her fingers crossed. Somehow, she convinced them that Speedy was lonely and it was cruel to have him alone in his tank all day while she was at school. They bought her story, and at the end of the week, Spring arrived. It seemed like they really liked each other, but there were little hints of trouble. One morning, Molly and I watched in horror as Speedy got out of his tank, fell off the desk, and walked out of the room muttering something about not wanting to share his tank. When Moozie got home from taking the kids to school, Speedy was standing by the back door! We couldn't believe it! Moozie scooped him up, put him back in the tank, lowered the water level and then smiled knowing she had outsmarted him. The problem is that when a turtle is motivated enough, they can do amazing things.

It happened about a month later, Moozie went in to feed them and only Spring was in the tank! She frantically looked everywhere, knowing a one-inch turtle cannot travel that far in a few hours. (She didn't realize he had been planning the escape for weeks, and had slipped out of the tank the night before.) We tried to tell him how foolish he was, and reminded him that Bailey could eat him if she found him, but he was determined to escape. Everyone was devastated, especially Katie. They spent two days with flashlights looking in every crack and crevice you can imagine, but no luck. After 5 days, they gave up. Moozie began worrying that he would die somewhere and start stinking which was not a pleasant thought.

Finally, something amazing happened! Dadzer was downstairs in the basement working, when he looked up and saw what looked like dog poop on the carpet. Normally, he would call Moozie for such an emergency, but she was outside. He slowly moved closer, and to his shock he found a very dehydrated, exhausted and half starving Speedy lying there. He had been gone for 12 days! We are still baffled at how he got down the basement stairs without injury, but apparently, turtles are quite sturdy.

After he was safely back in his tank, we had a long "chat" and he promised us that he is not going to attempt that again! As added protection, Moozie bought a lid for the tank the very next day so I don't think he'll be going anywhere anytime soon. Again, I have to say that guineas are the perfect pets, we never escape and are disease-free!

Speedy, rehydrated after 12 days of roaming free!

CHAPTER 8

The Birthday Party

In October, Katie was invited to a birthday party that a friend in her class was having. It was a carnival theme, and sounded like so much fun that Molly and I were sad to miss it! Katie had a blast with the face painting, cotton candy, pie throwing contest, and races but there was one event that really captured her attention. It was the goldfish toss! She tried and tried to get the ping pong ball to land in that little bowl, and was so discouraged when she didn't win a fish. But good news! The Mom and Dad said that anyone that wanted one could take a goldfish home; wasn't that lucky? For some reason, Moozie did not look that thrilled when she picked her up. "Katie, we are heading straight to the Toby Mac concert at Carowinds, what will this fish do in the car for 4 hours?" Katie was not the least bit worried about this detail and proceeded to ask the girl's father if she could take one home. (Ugh, Moozie sighed but smiled inside because everyone knows goldfish have short lives).

When Katie got her bag with the fish, "Goldy," she handed it to Moozie. Strange, she thought, the water seems awfully warm (next time maybe the dad shouldn't pack the fish to send home). They headed to Chick-fil-A but the more Moozie held the bag, the hotter she thought the water felt...way too hot for a goldfish. But what could they do? They only had the bag it came in...then a great idea popped into Katie's head! On the floor was a plastic cup, if they poured the fish into the cup the water would cool down while they were eating. What a perfect solution! So they transferred the goldfish, and headed in to enjoy dinner.

Well guess what? Fish must really hate hot water! When Moozie and Katie got back in the car the first thing they did was peek in the cup. Hmm, that's odd, it's empty! At the same time, they both looked down on the floor mat, and there under Katie's foot was a flapping goldfish. It never occurred to them that she would jump out of the cup just because it was hot! They put her back into the cup as quickly as they could and added an ice cube, but they both knew this was a lot of stress for a little fish.

The concert was great, all four of them had a fabulous time and forgot all about poor little Goldy until it was over. When they got back in the car, they were shocked to see she was still alive! Everyone sighed with relief and they headed home. At 10:30 PM they pulled in, and bring the new pet into the pet room for us to see. "Aren't you excited Sarah? Look at our new fish!" Katie beamed, she was so happy. We were lukewarm on this idea, but fish are definitely better than birds!

Sunday morning came, and sadly, it was funeral time at the Cones' house. Goldy never really had a chance. Katie cried and cried, and insisted she needed more fish to replace him. Moozie was still getting used to cleaning the turtle tank so she put her off as long as she could. Unfortunately, soon afterwards Katie received another $50 Petsmart gift card so there was not much she could say. Somehow Katie talked her into a tank, filter, lid, light, two fish and two frogs as a replacement for Goldy. I am telling you that free pets are very expensive. Katie was so happy because now she was up to twelve pets which even she said was enough. Moozie was ecstatic, but she still had two tanks, a bird cage, and a guinea cage to clean each week, as well as a fifty-pound puppy to chase after. Nothing productive ever gets done around here!

CHAPTER 9

Vet Visits and New Cages

On the first Saturday of each month, we visit Dr. Austin (assisted by Dr. Katie) for a full check-up. Katie has sticky notes she uses to guide her through a rigorous examination to determine if we have any unwanted conditions. After a brushing, and check of our temperature, we run through the checklist:

- No Lice
- No Ticks
- No Fleas
- Nails trimmed properly
- Excessive weight gain

Whoa…wait a minute, what was that last one? Excessive weight gain? Did she really check that box?

"Moozie, guess what? Sarah has gained too much weight and needs to have her carrots cut back!" Katie yells to her mom. Oh no, tell me Moozie won't approve of this, we love our carrots! Well the voice of reason comes in, and confirms that yes, we have been gaining weight lately, but we are also growing. She winks at us and whispers, "Don't worry, I'll sneak you some carrots when Katie's at school." It's just another reason that we love Moozie!

Luckily, this most recent visit leads to another of Katie's brilliant ideas. If we are growing that fast, it's probably time for a bigger cage. Slowly but surely, she begins to plant the seed with Moozie that an upcoming expense is imminent. All we hear from Moozie is "their cage is just fine." (We on the other hand believe a little more space would be nice but no one asks us.) Soon, Katie starts doing research on all the options, and convinces her mom that it probably makes sense to leave the small cage they have now in Texas for visits to the grandparents.

Well, somehow Moozie gets involved and picks what we all think is the perfect cage. It says right on the box, "created by guinea pig experts" so it must be the best! It goes on sale (Moozie is very cheap) and once the order is placed we wait anxiously for the big day. This new cage finally arrives and it has two compartments with a ramp connecting them. One compartment is for food, hay, water and the poop area and the other is for play and sleeping. The instructions say that Guineas generally only "eliminate" in the area where they eat and drink, so you only need to put litter in that area of the cage. Moozie is thrilled because litter is very expensive.

Ahhh, how pretty this new cage looks. We love it! We settle in while the family eats a nice relaxing dinner. When Moozie peeks her head in later she notices something strange, there is a little poop on the "sleep and play" part of the cage. *I guess they are getting used to it*, she thinks optimistically.

The next morning, more poop and now pee is in the wrong area, not a good sign. She heads back to the computer for more guinea research, and Moozie realizes she hasn't trained us properly. Apparently, every time we poop in the corner of the food area she is supposed to clap and praise us. We watch hysterically for several weeks as she does this, knowing all the while we are going to "eliminate" wherever we feel like it. I think the cage-inventing-guinea pig experts forgot we are rodents, and fooled a bunch of people. Well, this went on for quite a while until Moozie finally called it quits.

Uh oh, is that a poop in the food area?

We are now the proud residents of a large, double compartment cage, filled with litter in both areas. Moozie is very irritated and keeps muttering about how she is now spending twice as much on litter as before, but we think our health and hygiene are worth it.

In the end, we are very happy to have our great new cage. It even says it can hold up to three guineas but I just know what will never happen! (Moozie tore up that part of the box before Katie even got to read it.)

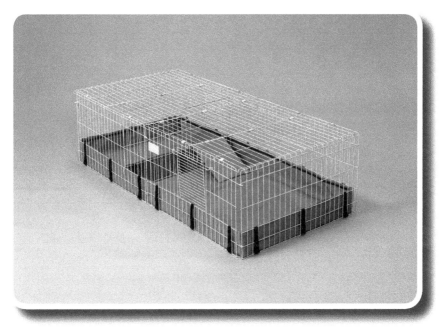

Our new double compartment cage!

CHAPTER 10

Bike Rides and Math Tests

Well, life rolled along for us and soon it was fall, the start of a new school year. Bailey was getting bigger each day, but I have to admit we kind of liked her! Katie continued to insist that we loved the activities she loved, such as bike rides and car trips. Every day after school she would put us in her bike basket and ride around the neighborhood for hours, it was quite a challenge to our nerves and stomachs! Often she would stop at someone's house to play and leave us in the basket, totally forgotten. Luckily Moozie was very good about checking in on her so we usually weren't forgotten for too long.

Katie holding me before riding to school!

Even though Katie was still as precocious as ever, she was slowly showing signs of growing up. One subtle change was she stopped calling her mom, "Moozie" and her dad, "Dadzers." That was a tough adjustment for everyone, and we still have a hard time referring to them as our Mom and Dad. Bailey remained Bubba throughout the winter though.

One day, Katie insisted that we should ride along to school with her to enjoy the scenery (not much scenery when you are wrapped tightly in a towel sitting on someone's lap, but that's a detail). Anyway, on these days we would get to hear the interactions that occurred on their way to school, and they were quite amusing to us Guineas. We just couldn't believe some of the things that came out of that kid's mouth!

On this particular day, Katie had a math test. Her mom was trying to be helpful by quizzing her the entire way to school on all her math facts and times tables. Katie was more interested in petting us than participating and made that very clear, but Moozie can be persistent too. Finally, we arrive at school after a twenty-five-minute car ride that we would have gladly skipped if given the opportunity! Anyway, as Katie was getting out of the car, she says very calmly, "Mom, you need to just take a DEEP breath and relax. You are way too wound up about my math test, this is only the third grade. It will all be fine, just go home and forget about it, and play with the pets and stop worrying! I'm not worried, why should you be?"

Katie got out of the car and we laughed, it was funny to think how upset we would get worrying about her, and Katie didn't care one bit about school! That kid truly lived for her pets, and we lived for her!

CHAPTER 11

Girls' Weekend

Well, whether we like it or not, every January, Moozie gets to go on a Girls' Weekend with all her friends from New Jersey. She gets to spend two days at the Hotel Hershey, eating unlimited chocolate and relaxing at the spa, while we suffer at home. Even though she loves the chance to get away, I know she misses and worries about us terribly. When she is gone, my kids are responsible for us which usually doesn't go smoothly. Often we are hungry, thirsty and frazzled when she gets home, but still she insists on going every year.

Moozie just got home last night, and so many things happened during her first twelve hours back that she had to let her friends know all about it. After the kids left for school, Moozie scooped me into her lap, gave me a few hugs and carrots, and then blasted out an email to her girlfriends. Luckily, she has a great sense of humor, or she might have headed back out the door for good!

Monday, January 14th
Hi Everyone,

 I miss you guys already; this weekend was so fun and relaxing. This year re-entry seemed extra crazy for some reason.

 I got home last night at 8:30 (instead of 5:15) but who doesn't want to hang out in Newark with a pigeon flying over your head for 3 hours? I told Jen I was going to catch it and bring it home for Katie, and I kind of think she thought I was serious which is disturbing.

Anyway, when I finally arrive home, Bailey was stuck to me like glue with the saddest eyes I'd ever seen. I thought it was sweet until I checked her water bowl, bone dry. Checked the two outdoor bowls, bone dry. I fill up the bowl, she drinks for six minutes without stopping, hmmmm...good start!

I head into the pet room to check on everyone, but the light bulb has burned out and requires a ladder. No problem, I'll wait until the morning. I lock up Bailey, and head to bed. At 6:30, I let out Bailey (who is crossing her legs from all the water at 9:00) and all 3 birds fly over my head towards the light in the hallway. They are gone, went straight to the basement, I'll have to get them soon. Wake up the kids, get them in the shower and start packing lunches. As I'm doing that, John comes in with a net and starts chasing the birds, he catches Little Anne, but she is biting his finger very hard, he is not happy. Blue is hiding on top of the refrigerator, no sign of Angel. I turn around and Bailey is holding 2 of Katie's stuffed animals that she just stole off her bed, but she drops them to chase Blue. Apparently she's some kind of bird retriever. At this moment, Katie walks in and says "Yesterday, my frog was alive, but now his leg is stuck in the filter." I say I'll check him later, (we are now down to 11 pets, but it was a nasty clean up).

I come back from school and spent 40 minutes running around with a net chasing both birds, Blue was in our Christmas tree that didn't get put away over the weekend. See picture. All birds are now back in their cage and have been grounded indef-

initely. I just can't wait to get our new puppy, Zoey in 12 days. We will then be back up to 12 pets, but who knows for how long.

You can't make this stuff up; I am so ready for next year! Only 364 more days!!!!

Love,
Texas T

Blue sitting in the Christmas tree, hiding from Bailey

CHAPTER 12

Zoey, the Absolutely Final Pet

It's mid-January now and things are finally returning to normal since Moozie is back from her trip! But I should probably back up a few months and fill you in on some developments. Remember how I said Bailey kept growing? Well she did, and Katie was not happy with this news one bit. Where was her cute little puppy? She felt completely ripped off but didn't know how to work on her parents.

She hatched a plan and started working on it during the fall; it started with just subtle hints here and there. She'd make little comments on how expensive a big dog must be compared to a small dog, etc. You get the idea, nothing overt just suggestions. One day, while they were at a softball game, one of the other mom's brought her brand new Schnoodle puppy for everyone to meet, wasn't that lucky? And guess what? They always stay puppy-sized, which is just ideal! Now that Katie had an idea, she began to research full throttle. As you can imagine, Katie is quite a whiz at shopping for pets. All she had to type was "North Carolina Schnoodle Breeders," and several popped up! This was easier than anyone thought.

First, she sucked Moozie in by asking her to retell stories of the Schnauzer she had growing up, didn't she just love her? What was her name? And on and on it went. Then she asks her mom, "Why do you think they invented a Schnoodle as a breed?" Moozie unwittingly answers that Schnauzers are great family dogs but not super smart, and when you cross it with a poodle you are supposed to end up with a really intelligent family dog. Katie thought this was perfect and asked Moozie to look at pictures online of how cute the puppies were (I shouted "NO" from my cage but no one ever listens to me!).

Pretty soon, it's October and Katie knows she has to take it up a notch, so one night when the parents go to dinner, she has the babysitter help her with her idea. It's an amazing idea! They make a poster with all the reasons why she should get a puppy for Christmas.

Of course, Moozie just laughs when she gets home but it doesn't seem very sincere which worries me quite a bit. As much as I'd like the distraction of another pet, I know her mom has too much on her plate to adequately care for another puppy. Bailey was only five months old for Heaven's sake! The good thing was Dadzer was totally against this crazy plan so I knew we were fairly safe.

Well, the family continues on with all the activities associated with fall like softball, bike rides, golf and, of course, the guinea pig Christmas picture. Surely, you've heard of that? It's like regular picture day taken to the extreme. Not just bows this time, but full-out costumes. We hate it but really have never gotten a vote.

Moozie thinks it's awful too, but says her Facebook friends just love us (whatever that means). You can see we are very photogenic, but that is absolutely beside the point!

Sarah and Molly, Merry Christmas! Sarah still wet from her bath.

Anyway, you are not going to believe this but after all that whining and manipulating from Katie, Moozie still held strong with her NO answer. We were so proud of her again! However, Katie wasn't deterred by a simple no. Instead, she decided to take the matter straight to Santa and let him deal with it. Why involve your unwilling parents? She knew she believed strongly enough to bring that puppy to their house, and guess what? Santa brought her Zoey (well actually a note that she'd be ready to leave her mom in January) but that was good enough for Katie. One more pet to add to the inventory, and this really was going to be the final, and I mean final pet ever! And seriously, isn't she cute?

CHAPTER 13

Grandparents and Construction Projects

After Zoey arrived, Katie started feeling a little guilty for us. She didn't have the time to devote to us like before; two puppies are a lot of work. Every time she walked by our cage and saw us cramped in our little Igloo, she felt just awful. Since she wasn't about to give up Zoey, she decided something needed to be done to make us feel important again. She began to think.

You have probably realized by now that Katie is not only strong-willed and goal-oriented, but luckily, she is also clever, creative and resourceful. All of these qualities will serve her well as an adult but they tend to be exhausting for Moozie. This time however was a little different, because this time Grandma and Grandpa were the unknowing targets.

I should back up a little, and tell you about Moozie's parents. They are really quite fabulous people and they genuinely love dogs and guinea pigs (no surprise there). I have heard that some grand-parents frown on grand-guineas coming for Christmas and taking up the entire laundry room, but not mine! They love it when we visit, and we love when they come too! Grandma just cries and hugs us when we leave; she just anxiously awaits our next visit.

Well, last week they arrived in Charlotte for a visit and Katie was so worried they would be bored while she was at school. She jumped on the computer for a little research on projects to keep Grandpa busy. Katie had just been to Petsmart and was admiring a wooden house for us, something a little bigger than our igloo (we were getting kind of cramped in there). Petsmart had a nice house, but it was $19 and nothing elaborate, so Katie insisted Grandpa could make something much nicer for less. So began the process.

Katie began frantically sketching her ideas; she wanted this house to be amazing and something we would be proud to call home. She decided we needed a double decker house, the bottom part would be for sleeping and a ramp would lead to the top that would serve as a hay loft and lookout area. It was beautiful, and Grandpa was totally on board with the project (he wasn't given a vote, but that is beside the point). Anyway, off to Home Depot they went where they picked the highest quality wood you could purchase. We wanted this to last for years and years, no shortcuts allowed. (Not only is Grandpa nice but he is an engineer as well).

They went to the workshop and started cutting and gluing for hours at a time. Katie brought us along so we could be a part of the building process which really heightened our anticipation. We were ready to move in; there was only one tiny problem. Delays. When you ask an engineer to build a guinea pig house, it is not thrown together. This house was basically an Amish quality production, no nails to poke us (only glue) and all the joints were attached with pegs. The ramp had notches every few centimeters to make it easy for our claws to gain a foothold, he truly thought of everything. It took Grandpa about sixty hours to make that house, but we are totally worth it! Katie thought he should sell them online, but given that the materials were $45 and labor costs, Moozie decided most people wouldn't be willing to pay enough to make it feasible. No matter, what did we care? We now have an amazing house to live out our golden years in, and we couldn't be happier.

You can see from the picture how amazing this is, but the best part was that I now had a place all to myself. I would often sneak upstairs in the hay loft and write down my thoughts for the book, it was so nice. Molly never knew what I was doing up there, which made it more special for me.

CHAPTER 14

We're Moving Again!

We had lived in Charlotte for just over two years, when Katie's dad got a new job. Normally this would be a great thing, but this new job happened to be in Texas. The parents were very happy because they were moving back to their old neighborhood from six years ago, but we were not thrilled. We had grown up in Charlotte and it was the only home we knew.

The kids had no idea; they weren't home during the day, eavesdropping like we were. I tried to warn Katie but she just didn't understand me. Moozie thought it would be a great idea to tell the kids at dinner. So one night in early November, she put the family's "You are Special" red plate in front of Dadzers. As Katie and Austin walked in, they looked at the plate warily and slowly sat down. "What is going on? Is it your birthday?" They asked.

Moozie excitedly began talking "We have some great news, Dad got a new job and he's very excited about it!" Austin said "That's great as long as we don't have to move, I absolutely love it here." Dead silence from Mom and Dad, then tears in Austin's eyes. "What, we're moving?" This was not going as planned. They quickly told them all the great reasons to move back to Texas, how they'd be closer to family, etc. but they just weren't buying it! They ran away from the table crying, and saying "I never want to see that stupid red plate again."

It was not a fun night at the Cones' house, Molly and I were a little worried too because we loved our pet room and hated the thought of leaving. Dadzer commuted back and forth for the next few months until it was finally time to start the moving process. The kids wanted to finish up the school year before leaving, so in April they listed the house. And great news! The first people that walked in put a contract on it, and they were willing to wait until early July to close, everything was working out so nicely. The parents frantically made plans; they got the kids enrolled in school in Texas, put a contract on a house there and were ready to move mid-summer. Everyone was happy (except for my kids!) and it all seemed to be working out so nicely.

The parents did so much work getting ready for the move; they took down all the pictures on the walls and started packing up all the fragile decorations. It was such a busy time for everyone; we hardly got any attention at all! We were trying to be understanding, but it was a very difficult time in both of our lives.

Then one day in late June the dreaded call came in. Two days before the house was to close, the people decided to back out of the contract! It was awful! As you can imagine, this was quite a shock, and soon all the happy vibes turned to worry vibes. That was one of my LEAST favorite months in the Cones' family. The kids, however, were thrilled that the sale fell through; now they got to spend the rest of the summer in Charlotte (kids don't worry about things that stress out parents).

Anyway, the house went back on the market, but this time, Moozie decided the pet room should really look like a homework room, she thought that would appeal to more people. She told us most people don't have a dedicated pet room, which seems crazy and impossible to believe! She had a horrible idea; she thought the pets should be relocated to the garage while the house went back on the market (and it was summertime!) We were so mad at her, and so were the birds! No one could believe it! The dogs were set up in the garage too, but they only had to be there during "showings" and were free to roam inside whenever they wanted to. It was so unfair!

It was during this chaotic time that it happened. The horrible, unthinkable thing happened. Remember how I said I wished the birds would just fly away one day? Well, to be honest I never really meant it, I kind of got used to them and we talked quite a bit through the cages. One day, Moozie rolled their cage out onto the driveway to clean it, and had no idea one of the four doors was unlocked. She accidentally jostled the cage, and boom the door opened when she wasn't looking. I told the birds to stay in the cage, I was yelling in fact, but they didn't listen one bit. All they saw were the beautiful trees and creek behind their backyard and they were gone in an instant! Moozie could not believe it, she called and called for them and even left the cage in the driveway for days thinking they'd come back. Sadly, they never returned.

Now Moozie was left with the awful job of telling Katie about it. In the end, she decided to do what any Mom would do, she stalled. She told Katie there wasn't room in the car for the birds so they were coming in the moving truck (which was half true since the cage was coming in the truck). Then she just hoped she'd forget all about the birds, do you think that happened?

CHAPTER 15

Our House in Texas

Well, it was time get back in the car for another 1,000-mile trip to Texas. Katie crammed us back into the cat carrier, Bailey was in the back (drooling and vomiting), Zoey was in Moozie's lap, and the turtles were under the seat in their travel container. It was quite a sight! After several days we made it to Texas, but since we hadn't sold our house we had to move into a temporary apartment.

The parents tried to make it sound like an exciting adventure, but we all missed our pet room (and the birds). We lived in this apartment for four months; it was a great time of "extreme togetherness" as Moozie called it. The joke in the family was the apartment was so small that the only place Zoey had to sit was on top of Bailey!

I'm not kidding when I say we had a small apartment, in fact our cage really had no proper place to sit. Sadly, they ended up shoving our cage in a dark, cramped corner and we were rarely visited or played with. There also wasn't room for the turtle tank, and after all that driving in the car with them, Katie wasn't about to let go of them! So she found a solution that was just brilliant. Her previous best friend, Taylor, still lived in their neighborhood, and they had a Red Ear Slider named Flash. He was absolutely huge compared to Speedy and Spring, and his tank was enormous! It was the perfect place to escape from the apartment, and we were very jealous of our turtle friends. We told Speedy to be on his best behavior while he was in the temporary tank, our family did not want to be embarrassed!

Well, I think Speedy tried to be good for a few weeks but then he went back to his old antics. Not only did he start escaping, but he also taught their turtle how to escape! The girls would watch Speedy climb on to Flash's back and sneak out, and then Speedy would wait for him to escape, leaving Spring alone in the tank. At first I think the other mom thought this was cute and amusing, but her patience soon wore out (as you can imagine!). You only need to find a turtle under your bed a few times for the fun to wear off. Our turtle was losing his welcome at their house, and we needed to get out of the apartment fast.

Finally, in September the house sold and the shopping for a new house began! We could see the light at the end of the tunnel, and we were ready for it! It was a great time for Moozie, but once again she was so busy that she often forgot to take care of us properly. Many times, she would come home from looking at houses to find Bailey gently reminding her that she hadn't been fed!

My family found a house in their previous neighborhood, and we were set to move in right before Christmas. What perfect timing! Molly and I couldn't wait to see our new room, we hoped it had windows and met all our rodent needs. That was when the troubling news came; there wasn't going to be a pet room. This new house was much smaller, so get this; they planned on putting our cage on the upstairs landing! Molly and I tried really hard not to act like spoiled brats about our new setup, but I'm not sure we were very successful. You can't imagine how much hay and litter we tossed out of the cage during those first few weeks out of spite. I'm a little embarrassed by our behavior now, but we were really mad about our new cage placement.

The other bad thing that happened during this time was the moving truck showed up with all the things that had been in storage for four months. Katie ran out to the truck to see the birds (poor thing, I think she really thought they'd be there after all this time) and there was only an empty cage. This did not go over well! Katie cried and cried, and said her Christmas was ruined. Of course, Moozie gave in and said they'd get another bird very soon, but not until after their trip to Grandma's house.

Katie recognized the guilt her parents were feeling and thought it was the perfect time to bring up an idea she'd been tossing around for a new pet. She began to tell Moozie how sad it was that they didn't have any snakes or lizards. Moozie doesn't have many rules about pets, but one thing she was adamant about was that she would never own a pet "that ate live food." Since lizards ate crickets, that fell right into this category and she said no way! As you can imagine, that didn't bother Katie one bit, she knew she had a few tricks up her sleeve.

Believe it or not, one of the things Katie asked for at Christmas was more gift cards to Petsmart.

Bailey and Sarah during the first month
in the new house

CHAPTER 16

Girls' Weekend and Bearded Dragons

Christmas was fun and relaxing as always (we love going to Grandma's house!) but we were happy to come home. Moozie wasn't because there were still about a hundred boxes left to unpack, and she was very tired of moving. Even though there was a million things left to do, Moozie still left a week later for her annual Girl's Weekend. Off to Hershey, PA for a relaxing time with twenty of her friends (she is so lucky!).

Dad was in charge and did all the usual things that Moozie hates, like movies with popcorn and extra butter, huge cokes, lots of hamburgers and fried chicken, you get the idea. This year was no different, except for a little idea Katie had. She began to think that maybe Dadzer would be more receptive to her idea of getting a bearded dragon, since they aren't really "Mom" pets. I mean they are kind of cute as babies, but they get ugly very quickly. And to top it off, they eat live crickets! This is going to be a tough sell, but as usual, Katie was armed with Christmas money and gift cards and ready to shop.

Soon they ended up back at Petsmart, this time shopping for a bearded dragon. Moozie certainly wouldn't have allowed this if she had been consulted, but she had done the unthinkable. She had been out all day shopping with her friends and was a little sleepy so she decided to rest for just thirty minutes. During that brief time, Katie and Dadzer texted her to see if she would mind if they got another pet, but she didn't reply. Obviously, Katie assumed her silence meant a yes, so they moved forward. By the time Moozie woke up, her phone had two new pictures on it, neither of them made her very happy! Pete had arrived at the Cones' house!

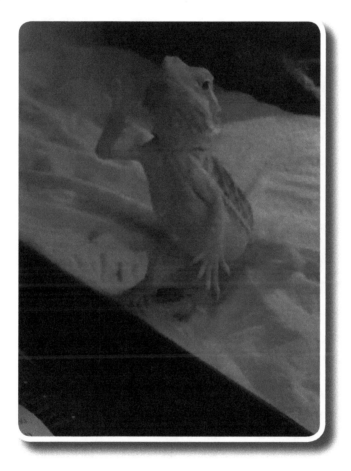

Thankfully Moozie made it back from her girls' trip, and began the process of bonding with Pete. This was a slower process than her other bonding experiences because she kind of thought he was ugly. She tried really hard, but honestly when you have a bearded dragon set up next to the two cutest Guineas in the world, what pet do you think you'd choose? I thought it'd be a good time to show you our set up on the landing so you can sympathize with the conditions we faced in this new house!

I can hear you saying that we are spoiled, but seriously moving to a landing from a pet room? Who wouldn't be put out?

I assume you are thinking that the bearded dragon replaced the birds, right? No way, Moozie is not that smart! She also got her another green bird (Little Anne 2) and they decided to put her cage in Katie's room. How special for them! We were stuck on the landing, but this bird gets the prime spot next to Katie's bed. It's probably a really good thing that Katie could not understand my squawking during those next few weeks, or I might have had soap in my mouth!

And after thinking about it, I realized it made sense from a safety perspective. Since Little Anne was allowed to fly around, it seemed logical that she was contained in a room, but it didn't seem fair. However, none of us were ready to tell Katie of another bird escape so we erred on the side of caution.

One good thing that came from Pete's arrival was the freeing of Speedy and Spring. Remember how they kept getting out of their cage? Well this poor behavior did not stop just because we moved into the new house! Apparently, they were not happy with their placement in the laundry room, and kept letting Moozie know by jumping out. It's much harder to get a turtle out from under a washer or dryer, so you can imagine the frustration level developing at our house. Around the same time, the fun was wearing off for Flash at Taylor's house as well. The girls hatched a plan to free the three turtles together. So one beautiful fall afternoon, they took all three turtles to the neighborhood lake. There were already about 100 similar turtles there so we knew they would just love it. And they did! They took off for the water and never looked back; I think Speedy was finally happy to have a huge place of his own. We were sad that night but knew they were in a better place.

CHAPTER 17

Tornadoes and Funerals

Today is a sad day, a very sad day. This is Molly, and you are probably wondering why I'm writing all of a sudden. I hate to enter the story and bring bad news right off the bat, but sometimes that is what life throws at you. Let me back up to yesterday and fill you in on what has happened.

It started out as a perfectly normal fall day, beautiful weather, not much on our agenda really, just some eating and relaxing. Everything was going great until Sarah started telling me she didn't feel well. I couldn't get her to come out of our house no matter what I tried and she wasn't eating or drinking. I kept shouting for my humans to take her to the vet, but no one heard me. It was the most terrifying day of my life. Sarah continued to get weaker and weaker, and desperately needed water but was too tired to get it. I tried to bring her some but that is very tough. Sadly I watched her deteriorate the entire day, and Moozie and Katie had no idea.

Finally around dusk, Sarah took her last breath. I could hardly breathe myself; she was my sister, my best friend, and my mentor. What would I do without her? Even though we had tons of other pets, none of them shared my cage or were my constant companion. I laid there waiting for Moozie to discover our loss. It took a few hours, but around bedtime Moozie remembered she hadn't tucked Katie in so she headed upstairs to give her one last kiss. As she walked up the final step, she said "Good night Sarah, good night Molly!" But this time Sarah didn't squeak back with her "good night" to Moozie, and I watched her stop in her tracks. She knew, absolutely knew in that instant that Sarah was dead. There was never one time that Sarah did not squeak back to Moozie, she was an amazing guinea (but you already know that!).

Slowly she opened our cage lid and called again, and again. With dread, I watched her lift the house to see Sarah's lifeless body lying there in the hay. Tears instantly filled her eyes with such sadness, both for her loss and for Katie. This was going to be an awful thing to tell her! She woke up Austin and had him help her clean our cage to make sure there weren't any germs that might harm me (she is so thoughtful!). They cleaned and scrubbed until almost 11 that night and she gave me an extra hug before trying to settle me down for bed.

Moozie tossed and turned for hours that night, she was so upset for Katie. She kept having dreams that an ambulance was bringing Sarah to the vet and saving her. The ambulance seemed to go on for hours in her dream until finally she woke up and realized it wasn't a dream. There wasn't an ambulance; it was actually the tornado alarms going off! She had been gone from Texas for so many years that she had forgotten all about them. Instantly, she checked her phone to see if there was a tornado in the area, and there didn't seem to be. She decided to lie there a little longer and see what happened but soon the alarm elevated in urgency. Now, there was actually a voice saying "take cover immediately" and she decided this might be serious! Moozie ran upstairs and got Katie, Austin and both dogs and huddled in the closet under the stairs, it was now 3 a.m. (Good time to mention that Dad was out of town for all this fun!)

After a few minutes in the closet, Katie began to wake up and realize what was going on, mainly that Sarah and Molly were upstairs and in danger! "Mom, we need to go get Sarah and Molly and bring them down here!" Imagine what was going through Moozie's mind? How do you tell your daughter at 3 in the morning, while huddled in a closet avoiding an imminent tornado, that her beloved guinea pig is actually in the freezer awaiting a funeral? She did what any mom would do in that situation, she lied. "Katie, they are okay, the weatherman said that dogs are the only pets that need to be in the closet, the guineas are fine upstairs." Somehow Katie bought that story, and the news was delayed until the next day.

After the tornado warning passed by, we all tried to get some sleep. I think Moozie and I both tossed and turned all night, missing Sarah. In the morning, everyone was tired, and running very late for school. Katie hardly had time to eat, much less play with her pets, so thankfully she never checked on us. Everyone knew school would be a waste if Katie found out about Sarah in the morning. She had to learn the news eventually, and after school her mom told her about Sarah. I don't need to go into the details here, but you can imagine what it was like in our household for a few weeks after that. Even Bailey was sad! She loved Sarah like we all did, and the next day I tried to give her my biggest hug and snuggle but it wasn't the same, they had such a special bond.

We all knew Katie was especially sad about Sarah because this time, and only this time, she didn't even ask for a replacement pet. There was no pet that could ever replace Sarah.

Bailey and Molly, the day after Sarah died,
consoling each other.

CHAPTER 18

Bailey the Agility Dog

After Sarah died, so many things changed around our house. It was like all of the fun had gotten sucked right out of the air. Katie finished sixth grade and began to get interested in new things. She was playing volleyball constantly, and as active as ever. Pete continued to grow, he got fatter every month and Moozie really struggled to "love" him. He seemed to constantly be shedding, and his cute little poops quickly became large piles of vileness. Not to mention the effect of the heat lamp on that smell, it was just gross. I was ready for a new neighbor!

Katie still loved horses, and tried to ride every week. She rode English and jumped, but still dreamed of being a barrel racer in her spare time. The barn that taught barrels was so far away that it just wasn't possible to go every week. One interesting thing that came out of the English jumping was Katie's love of a new sport. She began setting up jumps in the backyard and running over them on all fours. This was fun for a few days, but she needed something better. I remember the day well; Bailey, Zoey and I were all in the yard watching her jump when Katie suddenly turned around. You could see her look at Bailey and the light bulb just went off in her mind! Bailey was going to become an agility dog!

Zoey and I watched in amazement as Bailey went from a pampered pet to a working dog within a matter of weeks. Soon Katie was up training with her at 6 a.m. before the summer heat, and again long into the evenings. She began making a special diet to help Bailey focus and calm her muscles. She bought a Back on Track jacket that Bailey wore at night to ease any stiff joints. And mostly, Katie began begging neighbors for work to have money for agility equipment.

She was working her three to four hours a day, all summer and into fall. Grandpa came back to town and was forced to make a teeter and three jumps, Dadzer had to make a regular jump, a tire jump and weave poles and Moozie helped with the online ordering. It was quite a family affair. Zoey and I were observers, and Austin pretty much ignored the entire experience but it was still fun.

Katie had already decided this needed to be more than just a hobby, she knew Bailey had something special and they could do great things together. She researched agility training centers and found one that was close to home. After a few phone calls she had their first private lesson set up (obviously at Moozie's expense) and the training began in earnest. I'm a little proud to say this, but Katie really has a way with animals. The trainer was very impressed with how much Katie and Bailey had accomplished in such a short time, as it usually takes years to get to this point. Bailey was able to skip all the introductory classes and go straight to the ongoing Novice category, which was quite a feat! Moozie was happy because this saved a lot of money, but that is just the way she is.

Anyway, Katie's trainer suggested that she enter Bailey in an upcoming Charity show to see how they would do. Katie was ecstatic! She quickly filed for a Junior Handler number with the AKC, and then got Bailey registered with the AKC (Moozie had never seen a reason to do this before). She was ready for her first show; it was going to be in Fort Worth which was just an hour away. We were all so eager, and I couldn't wait for them to get back to tell me all about it.

When the first event came, Katie had already walked the course and warmed up Bailey, it was show time. Unfortunately, we soon became painfully aware of how much of a Golden Retriever Bailey really is. The clock started, Bailey took the first jump with ease.... and then...ran off! She had so much fun running around the ring, stopping to say hi to all the judges, trying to get bystanders to pet her.

She had a blast, Katie did not! She could feel her chances of winning slipping away.

The parents were so proud of her though, she gathered up Bailey (with the assistance of two judges) and regrouped. She never once threatened to quit or go home from embarrassment; she just got ready for the next event. There were still four more events; and Katie was determined. The next two were slightly better but still not good enough to qualify. The fourth event was only tunnels, and for the most part Bailey did great, she only stopped a few times to bark at someone. She actually had a qualifying run but her time was too slow to place. The final event was JWW, or jumps with weaves, and everyone was nervous to see how she would do! She had a rough start, but soon got it together and ended with a really good run. Good enough to place third out of eighteen dogs! It was such a great day for both of them, I was so proud when they told me about it that night.

What a great day for both of them! The very next morning Katie started seventh grade, and tried out for the school volleyball team. She made it! I was so happy for her but a little worried about what this would mean for me, it seemed she was getting interested in so many things and I still craved attention. Moozie still plays with me, and lets Little Anne out of her cage almost every day to fly around, but I missed Katie and Sarah. They made sure I had time most days to hang out with the dogs and play in the backyard, but nothing was the same.

Carrot time with Bailey and Zoey....

CHAPTER 19

Goodbyes (and Hello?)

Life rolled along as it always does, and a few weeks later it was time for Bailey's second agility show. This one was more official, it was an AKC sponsored show in Oklahoma City, on indoor turf this time. Bailey trains on indoor turf so we thought Bailey would win for sure! Just Moozie and Katie went this time, and they turned it into a girls' weekend of shopping, eating and taking Bailey to the dog park. The morning of the show was an exciting morning; they woke up in OKC that August day to the strongest earthquake ever felt in the state. What a way to start your day! Bailey was petrified by the way the hotel shook and the beds moved and told me all about it, it really threw her off for the entire day. Not the best way to start preparing for an important agility show!

They got there early so Katie could prepare her, and try to settle her down. They had almost 4 hours before her first event and the suspense was killing everyone.

Bailey warming up before her event, she just flies!

Much to Katie's dismay, Bailey had some good parts and bad parts to her runs that day; she did great on the jumps but kept looking for people to pet her at every turn. That kind of friendliness is really frowned upon in agility trials, and sadly this time she didn't even qualify. Katie was distraught; she thought it was going to be much easier to keep winning.

But as usual, Katie wasn't deterred by these slight failures. She came home and told me her plan. She was going to tell her parents she'd be willing to part with Pete if only she could get a Border Collie puppy. I'm pretty sure Moozie is smart enough to realize that a puppy is much more work than a bearded dragon, but Katie was certain no one would doubt her. She helped her mom put an ad in the local neighborhood website announcing a free "Adorable Bearded Dragon and cage" to a good home. Now they just needed to wait for all the offers to roll in, I'm not sure used, slightly obese lizards are in high demand but we shall see!

At the same time, Katie began researching breeders, talking to people at shows, going to pet adoptions, anything she could think of. She told her parents if she made straight A's, she'd spend all her money on a puppy. This is probably one of the few times her parents were hoping she wouldn't do well in school!

As I'm writing this final chapter, I realize how old I'm getting, almost 5 now. Certainly I won't be around much longer and there are so many things I'd love to know. Does Katie go on to play college volleyball? Will she really become a veterinarian? Or a dog trainer? Will Pete find a new home? And most importantly, will Katie ever talk her parents into yet another pet, a puppy no less?

I already decided I'm heading into retirement, if they get a puppy than he can write the next book, I hear Border Collies have lots of energy. And finally, if they get another puppy it better not bother me...ha!

ABOUT THE AUTHOR

Theresa's love of pets started at age 5 when her family brought home Bitsy, a Miniature Schnauzer puppy. Soon afterwards, their family moved to Texas and began accumulating more pets over the years, including parakeets, guinea pigs, rabbits, snakes, lizards, hamsters, gerbils, rats and finally, Angel. Angel became one of the great loves of Theresa's teenage years. She was a rather ugly "mutt" that they rescued from underneath a picnic table at a rest area in West Texas on a family vacation. Her ugliness was offset by her incredible spirit and undying loyalty, and she forever changed the way Theresa viewed animals. Angel was part of the dowry that Theresa brought into her marriage to John, and he was obviously thrilled to have Angel live out her golden years with the newlyweds.

After graduating from college, Theresa spent 15 years as a 401k consultant in the retirement industry before retiring to have kids (and pets). She has been married to John for 27 years and lives in the Dallas area with their children, Austin and Katie. She still has Bailey and Zoey, but she recently added another puppy to the mix, a Border Collie named Dash!

CPSIA information can be obtained
at www.ICGtesting.com
Printed in the USA
LVHW071804231020
669660LV00016B/1356